Parrots
Amazing A
For Youn

By Zahra Jazeel

Mendon Cottage Books

JD-Biz Publishing

Download Free Books!

http://MendonCottageBooks.com

Read More Amazing Animal Books

Purchase at Amazon.com

Download Free Books!

http://MendonCottageBooks.com

Table of Contents

Introduction

If you happen to visit a zoo in your childhood, I am pretty sure that you must have been mesmerized by the beauty of parrots and intrigued by the different varieties found in that enclosure. If a zoo could hold such an amazing collection, imagine the spectacular shows the parrots may put up in the wild apart from finding rare species in their very own natural habitat. What a wonderful sight it would be!

Especially when it comes to bird watching, parrots are a real treat to watch because of their spectacular shades of colors and their vivid behavioral patterns. Whether it is big, medium sized or large, parrots are special in their own way.

Parrots are real entertainers. There is no doubt about that. You may know that parrots can 'talk'. But how is that possible? Do you know why they 'talk' and what helps them 'talk'? Did you know that some parrots have some personality in them and require attention? Fascinating isn't it?

Come join us as we explore the world of parrots, where we will be learning about different parrot varieties, their behavior and most importantly – why and how do they 'talk'.

About Parrots

Parrots are colorful birds found mostly in tropical and subtropical regions in the world. There are more than 300 species in total. Now that's a lot of variety for a bird. The greatest diversity of parrots exist in Australasia, Central America, and South America.

Interestingly, when it comes to size, parrots are the only birds with the most variable sizes as they range from small, medium, large or somewhere in between.

The lifespan of a parrot is roughly about 20-75 years depending on their species. Some have even reported to have lived more than 75 years in the wild. Mostly, parrots live in flocks as social birds. Just like human beings communicate with one another through speech, parrots are known to communicate with each other by a series of loud screeching and squawking sounds. Recently it was revealed that baby parrots are given names and the little ones use the names to identify themselves and others to communicate effectively with one another.

Though some parrots build ordinary nests, others prefer their homes to be in holes of trees, rock cavities, ground tunnels and even in termite mounds.

Parrots are highly intelligent unlike some other birds and could be trained to perform tricks or imitate sounds. Some parrots are even said to have followed their owners like puppies when they are trained. So the next time you pay a visit to the pet shop, don't forget to check on parrots!

Features of Parrots

Just by looking at a parrot, we can identify many of its physical features. Parrots usually weigh from 0.6- 1.6kg and they are 3.5" to 40" tall depending on their species. A closer look at a parrot will reveal its cuteness and adorability in an instant. Some parrots are unicolored while some others like macaws are multicolored.

Each parrot species tend to have unique personalities. For example, cockatiels are quite nippy while Alexandrine parakeets demand attention when required. Parrots have a keen sense of hearing and sight which helps them escape from danger or to find food. The pupils of parrot's eyes dilate when it feels threatened or excited. The eyes are small and positioned on either side of its head which allows them to have a clear vision covering a wide scope.

A distinct feature found in all parrots is the presence of zygodactyl feet. Zygodactyl is the presence of 4 toes in a foot, 2 pointing forward and the rest pointing backwards. This feature helps parrots in having a firm grip when resting on branches or to hold any food when eating. They also have a strong pointed beak to crack open nuts or hard shells in fruits. Now you wouldn't want a bite from a parrot because that could be pretty painful.

Just like humans having a preference on using right or left hand to do most of their work, parrots have proven to show this ability in a research conducted on Australian parrots. These parrots demonstrated their distinct 'handedness' through their feet.

Some parrot species like cockatiels and cockatoos have a mobile crest on their head which adds to their beauty as well as charisma.

Where parrots live

Parrots live in all tropical and subtropical continents across the world. They prefer warm climates in general. This explains why a great number of species are found in Australasia and South America. It is important to note that certain endemic species are found in some Caribbean and Pacific islands. Though parrots are widely seen in rain forests, surprisingly some are even found in cities and suburbs as well.

Over the past few years, many parrots have been introduced to areas having temperate climates and the parrots have successfully established stable populations in some regions of America including New York. This was a step taken to make the parrots adapt to different regions and face challenges successfully.

Some parrots are sedentary but some are fully migratory. Macaws for instance are found commonly in Mexico. Though cockatoos are native to Australia, New Guinea and Indonesia, 7 different species are found in Philippines and Solomon islands apart from New Guinea and Indonesia.

Feral parrots are parrots living in non-native environments. A flock of feral parrots can be formed if they escape in mass quantities while importing them from airports or even quarantine facilities. If you think releasing a pet parrot can contribute in forming a feral population, you are wrong. This does not happen because the captive birds do not have the skills to survive unlike wild birds. However, there are instances where pet parrots having escaped or released have joined a flock of feral parrots successfully.

Diet of Parrots

What do you think is the diet of parrots? Only fruits and seeds? Well, think again. A parrot's diet is made up of fruits, seeds, pollen, buds, nectar and insects. Some of you may not believe that parrots consume insects. Not all species consume insects but some do. Here's an example to change your mind. Gold-winged Parakeets prey on water snails while some species of cockatoos feed on grubs. It may sound disgusting. But it is true. Many species also consume nectar when it is available. Hence parrots are omnivores, which means they eat both plant and animal matter.

Macaws and cockatoos diet mainly consists of seeds. From their strong and relatively large beak it is quite possible to conclude that their bills have evolved to crack open hard nuts and seeds. Parrots use their feet to grip their food while eating. If you happen to stand close to a parrot having nuts or seeds, you might be able to hear that sharp crisp and crackly sounds emitted by the bird.

Parrots are medics in natural world. Since seeds contain poison most of the time as a self-defense mechanism, parrots are cautious when having seeds. They make sure to remove any seed coat or fruit parts containing such chemicals prior to consumption. They also have an amazing habit of consuming clay because it helps in releasing minerals and absorbs toxic compounds from the inside. In simple terms, clay is used as a cleanser.

Intelligent Skills- mimicry and Speech

Parrots are smart animals. They have amazing vocal skills and known to imitate or mimic certain sounds or even human speech when tamed. A parrot species known as the African Greys are far superior to other species due to its ability to imitate and mimic sounds clearly. Wild African Greys are observed to have imitated other birds. Quite a bunch of pranksters, aren't they? Though the second prize for the best imitators in the parrot world goes to some Amazon parrots, many other wild parrots have not been spotted imitating other bird species.

The most interesting fact is that parrots do not have vocal cords. They form sounds by expelling air through their syrinx. Syrinx is the voice organ in birds just like larynx for humans. When you look closer at a talking parrot, you may be able to see the movement of their tongue during speech. This is because these birds use their tongues to shape sounds to enhance clarity. This proves vital when forming complex vowel sounds or consonants. The movement of tongue less than a millimeter can also affect the sound quality profoundly according to some researchers.

Parrots as Pets

Parrots are great companions to have as pets. They have the ability to take off your stress and boredom at once. This explains why they are the third most popular pets in America. Parrots in general require love, attention and care when rearing and may build trust and interact with humans when tamed properly. The most common species kept as pets include macaws, Amazons, cockatoos, African Greys, lovebirds and cockatiels.

Parrots tend to bite or show aggression when it feels threatened or mishandled. Some large species of parrots require a bigger cage and a supply of toys to keep them busy. In general, small parrot species like lovebirds and budgies have a shorter life span of 15-20 years while larger species such as macaws and Amazons have longer life spans of over 75 years.

The intelligence of a parrot depends mainly on how quick they learn new tricks and mimic sounds. A pet parrot could be trained very well to mimic human sounds or animal sounds and even sing for a tune. Some pet owners have even trained their parrots to dance to the beat of a song or perform tricks. Positive reinforcement is the key. Giving a treat if the bird does what he's told will make them repeat the same behavior again. Some parrots are even thought to have identified different moods of their house owners before responding.

Some parrots are trained to perform for an audience, mainly to kids as entertainment. Though some of the well trained parrots freeze looking at the cameras, some perform fearlessly. If you had the opportunity to go to a parrot show, don't miss it. It is always a wonderful experience to watch them perform enthusiastically.

Love Birds

Lovebirds are cute and adorable creatures. They are small in size and weigh less than 0.1kg. The normal lifespan of a lovebird is 10-15 years. There are so many different species of lovebirds like the pied lovebirds, violet love birds, Dutch blue lovebirds and orange face lovebirds. As you might have guessed, they are named according to their color mutations.

Lovebirds are relatively easy to house because of their smaller size. When many of these are kept together, it is a common sight to see them all snuggling together. Though they look very tiny, they do have the personality of a parrot. When reared, they will get so friendly that they might even dance on your shoulders. They love to spin and hang on toys or pull out the buttons from your shirt.

Some people think that lovebirds should be reared only in pairs. But this is a misconception. Lovebirds could be reared in singles or pairs. If you rear them as a single bird, it may bond more with you. However if you wish to give him a companion, that would not harm any of his social interactions.

Lovebirds do possess some of the intelligence or abilities of larger parrots. Sometimes they require 'gentle dominance training' used in larger parrots.

Parakeets

Parakeet means 'long tail'. Their sizes range from small to medium. The average lifespan of a captive parakeet is between 5 to 10 years. But some live well more than that. Parakeets are swift fliers and are very good at evading human hands. They are intelligent and could be trained well. The Guinness Record for the largest documented parrot vocabulary is held by a tiny blue parakeet named Puck though some may think it is an African Grey parrot. In the wild, parakeets search for food during cool hours of the day and seek protection from the midday heat under shady trees and bushes.

The most common parakeet which was discovered in 1891 is called the 'Budgie' or English parakeet. They are the most popular breed of pets in America. The Ring-necked Parakeet is a species native to Africa and Asia. It has become feral in many cities and even kept as pets. Many parakeet species of different varieties are sold as pets commercially. The budgerigar is the third most popular pet in the world. It is small and loves exploring its surroundings.

Parakeets are also great whistlers like cockatiels and can become hand-tamed. They also can mimic sounds and words. There are 2 basic types of budgerigar parakeets. They are the English 'budgie' and the American 'budgie'. When compared to an American 'budgie', the English 'budgie' is quite docile. Generally, parakeets love to bathe or play in the water. They enjoy climbing and chewing on small toys.

Each parakeet is unique on their own. New Zealand is home to several exotic parakeets. These birds are graceful and make great pets for first time bird owners. They are also very sociable and attention seekers. Apart from the budgies, several other species like Alexandrine, Indian Ring-neck and Sun Conures are also known as parakeets.

Cockatiels

Cockatiels are small parrots originally from Australia. But all the cockatiels sold in America as pets are from captive breeding stock since Australia placed a ban on exporting cockatiels in 1894. Cockatiels are members of the cockatoo family. This explains why they have a crest above their head just like cockatoos.

They are cuddly and undemanding. There are several varieties in their colors. Cockatiels are easy to train and bond with their owners quickly. The possibility of them talking is much higher when they are hand fed.

Cockatiels can whistle very well and the males are even capable of learning how to talk. The average lifespan of cockatiels is from 12- 20 years and sometimes they can live upto even 30 years. Though cockatiels can be a little nippy, they are a great choice for first time bird owners. In the wild, the males have more yellow around the face with brighter color than the females. But various other colors like silver, pearl and cinnamon are produced due to domestic breeding.

Cockatiels are friendly birds and they get along well with other species of birds apart from parrots. If proper attention is not provided, they can develop "psychological feather picking" to relieve boredom or loneliness. When grooming, these birds use a powder which is present on their feathers. Some human beings with allergies are quite sensitive to this powder and should be careful when purchasing a cockatiel as they could be present anywhere a cockatiel has spent time.

Cockatoos

Cockatoos could be identified easily as they possess a crest of feathers above their head which could be raised or retracted voluntarily. The size of a cockatoo ranges from about 12 to 27 inches. Diet of a cockatoo includes vegetables, fruits and grains. Nuts could be used as a treat when training. Though there are so many species in cockatoos, they could be divided mainly into 2 depending on their size. The smaller species include the lesser sulfur crested cockatoo and the Goffin's cockatoo. The moluccan, umbrella and the great sulfur crested cockatoos are the larger ones.

Though cockatoos can live up to 80 years or more depending on their species, sadly many die younger than this in captivity. Cockatoos are very friendly and affectionate. They bond with their owners very closely and become depressed or develop neurotic behaviors when neglected. As a result, they require a lot of time and affection. Though they are not well known to mimic speech, they have pretty good vocal abilities. They're playful and mischievous too. Since cockatoos love to destroy things by chewing, a regular supply of toys like softwood toys, rope toys and cardboards are a necessity.

Cockatoos can be very loud and excitable. They raise their crest when they are happy, excited, startled or agitated. It's a beautiful display. Some cockatoos have colored crests which are a magnificent display when raised. In wild, they are used for communication and to ward off predators. If a cockatoo raises it's crest they look impressive showing off their bigger size.

African Greys

African Greys have grey feathers as the name suggests and a strong black beak. They are native to the Western and Central African rainforests. The diet of an African Grey consists of fruits, seeds, leafy vegetables and sometimes snails. In general, there are 2 subspecies. They are the Timneh African Grey parrot and the Congo African Grey parrot. The latter is quite large in size than the former. African Greys are known to be very intelligent among the parrots because of their ability to mimic and learn new things fast.

In fact, the cognitive development of these birds are said to resemble that of chimpanzees and dolphins which are considered to be highly intelligent in the animal kingdom. Hence this could be the secret of its smartness.

African Greys reared as pets are known to have mimicked human speech, house appliances and even house pets like cats or dogs. The most impressive thing about their imitation is the clarity of sounds and in some cases, the ability to understand what the words meant. The most sensational African Grey who was popular for the last few years was Alex. Alex was a subject in an avian language experiment conducted by Dr. Pepperberg. Alex was so intelligent that he could identify what most human words meant, identify big or small objects, colors, sizes, matter and even count or add up small numbers. Though he died at the age of 31, most of them bred in captivity have a long lifespan.

African Greys are very sociable and love toys. In general, males are longer than females. The captive bred Timneh African Grey parrot is said to be less agitated than a Congo African Grey parrot when surrounded by strangers. It also learns to speak earlier than a Congo. Apart from their impressive mimicry, these birds could distinguish a large number of voices which is truly fascinating.

Macaws

Macaws are beautiful birds with colorful feathers. They are the largest among all the parrots having big hooked bills which are very useful to crack open nut pods or to consume seeds and fruits. There are around 16 different species ranging in size. Their wings are long and pointed which helps them fly with great speed. Their tails could exceed their body length or remain the same length as their body.

These birds are found in Central and South America. Macaws are bred as pets for their beauty and splendor. They are intelligent and social animals requiring a great deal of time and attention from their owners. Some species of macaws include the blue and gold macaw, scarlet macaw and the hyacinth macaw. Some other species like the yellow collared macaw and the Hahn's macaw are mini macaws which are quite harder to find.

With proper nutrition and care, a large macaw could live up to 50 years though mini macaws are expected to live less than that. Macaws can be very noisy and screech loudly. They do mimic but it is not as clear as African Greys or Amazons.

When choosing a cage for a macaw, it is best to make sure that the cage is strong enough to withstand the strength of its beak. A cage made of stainless steel is an ideal type for this purpose.

Parrots in various cultures

Many might think that parrots are used as pets only at present. But they were reared as pets long before. Parrot feathers were used for decoration and various cultural ceremonies in the good old days. However, in some parts of the world, such practices continue even till today.

In ancient Peru, the Moche people worshipped birds and parrots were often depicted in their art. Hence parrots were considered to be sacred. Even in

Buddhist scriptures, parrots were popular. An ancient story relates that when a forest caught fire, a parrot carried water to try and put out the fire and the ruler of heaven was so touched by its act that he sent rain to extinguish the fire.

Today, parrots are used to symbolize nations. For example, the national bird of St. Vincent and the Grenadines is the St. Vincent parrot and the parrot in a Dominican flag symbolizes the yearning for greater heights and aspirations.

Fictional parrot films like 'Paulie' and 'Rio' are made today while some companies opt for producing magazines or articles about parrots and their conservation. Few years back, Alex the African Grey parrot was an internet sensation stealing the spotlight due to his intelligence.

From the Aesop's Fable, "The parrot and the cat", Ovid the Roman poet's "The Dead Parrot' and the Dead Parrot Sketch of Monty Python, we can conclude that parrots did exist in many cultures.

Conservation of parrots

If you think all parrot species are well and safe, you're wrong. More than any other group of birds, parrots are said to be widely exploited. Many parrot species are threatened and several others are extinct. According to the IUCN (International Union for Conservation of Nature), 16 species are considered as Critically Endangered while 130 are listed as Near Threatened. There are several reasons why these birds are declining.

Habitat loss and trapping of wild parrots for pet trade are some of the causes. In certain parts of the world, some species of parrots are hunted for their beautiful feathers and food. There are also instances where parrots are killed as agricultural pests. Once, thousands of birds were killed when Argentina offered a bounty on Monk Parakeets. However, this did not affect the overall parrot population greatly.

Today, due to the measures taken to protect the habitats of some rare and charismatic species, several of the less charismatic species in the same ecosystems are also protected as a result. There are many active organizations which are dedicated in conserving parrot populations in the wild. An international organization known as the World Parrot Trust is one fine example. This organization produces magazines to create awareness and extend their support to worthwhile projects with the aim of conserving parrots. They also raise funds through donations.

Many projects such as these have become a success on many occasions.

Fun facts about parrots

Parrots have entertained human beings as pets from a very long time. They were even reared by some famous historical figures in the past. Want to know who these parrot owners were? King Henry VIII, one of the famous kings in the British history and Winston Churchill, former prime minister of England during the Second World War. Even Andrew Jackson and Napoleon were said to have reared parrots!

Parrots in the wild screech and squawk loudly as a way of communication.

The smallest parrot is the Pacific Parrotlet and the largest is the Hyacinth macaw.

There are instances where parrots kept as pets have learnt to sing opera.

Parrots in the wild are always busy playing, foraging and screaming. Hence a parrot should not be left alone in a cage ignored. They need stimulation to stay active, happy and healthy.

Parrots rank among the top when it comes to illegal pet trades.

A tail wag in a parrot is equivalent to a human giggle.

Some parrots like cockatoos, African Greys and Amazons play tricks on humans for enjoyment. They might signal they're friendly but when approached by a hand might bite. This is a way of amusing themselves with no true intention of harming the others.

Cockatoos move their heads up and down or wiggle their tongues if they are happy seeing someone or something.

Author Bio

Fathima Zahra Jazeel

Was born in Sri Lanka and completed her G.C.E Advanced Level in the Bio Science stream. She completed her BTEC Level IV Edexcel Professional Diploma in Teaching in the year 2013 and currently works as a teacher while following the BTEC Level V Edexcel Professional Diploma in Advanced Teaching leading to a professional degree. Her passion for journalism made her engage in writing for both local as well as international newsmagazines.

Her family had been rearing parrots as pets for decades which motivated her to be a local voluntary social worker to create awareness about conserving animals in the wild.

Download Free Books!

http://MendonCottageBooks.com

Purchase at Amazon.com

Website http://AmazingAnimalBooks.com

Horses
For Kids

Amazing Animal Books
For Young Readers
By John and
Annalee Davidson

Ponies
For Kids

Amazing Animal Books
Rachel Smith

Ten Amazing
Horses
For Kids

Nature Books for Kids
JD-Biz Publishing
K. Bennett

Akhal-Teke
"The Golden Horse
of the desert"
For Kids

Nature Books for Kids
JD-Biz Publishing
K. Bennett

Suffolk-Punch
"The Gentle Giant"
For Kids

Nature Books for Kids
JD-Biz Publishing
K. Bennett

Shires
"The great Horse"
For Kids

Nature Books for Kids
JD-Biz Publishing
K. Bennett

Colonial Spanish
"Horse of the Americas"
For Kids

Nature Books for Kids
JD-Biz Publishing
K. Bennett

Canadian
"The Little Iron Horse"
For Kids

Nature Books for Kids
JD-Biz Publishing
K. Bennett

Cleveland Bays
"History and Future"
Horses For Kids

Nature Books for Kids
JD-Biz Publishing
K. Bennett

Our books are available at

1. Amazon.com

2. Barnes and Noble

3. Itunes

4. Kobo

5. Smashwords

6. Google Play Books

Download Free Books!

http://MendonCottageBooks.com

Publisher

JD-Biz Corp

P O Box 374

Mendon, Utah 84325

http://www.jd-biz.com/

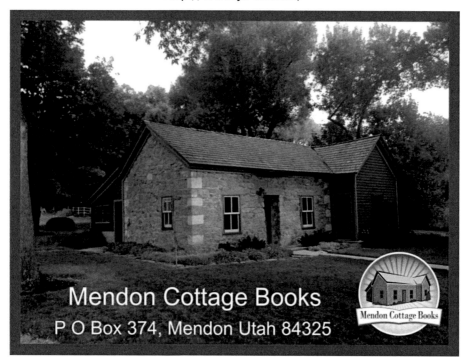

Made in the USA
San Bernardino, CA
16 May 2016